Every Day Crepes Recipes

The Complete Guide for Delicious, Mouthwatering Crepe Recipes

Ranae Richoux

Legal Disclaimer

Table of Contents

Culinary Canary on Facebook!

Want more free Culinary Canary eBooks? Like our Facebook page and not only will you be the first to download the newest books FOR FREE as we release them, you'll also get some of Culinary Canary's Best Sellers for free too! Not only will you be the first to download any new books, you'll also receive plenty of BONUS content, including contests and input, to make it more than worth your while. The provided Facebook link will take you directly to our Facebook page and will allow you to receive all the benefits immediately:

https://www.facebook.com/CulinaryCanary

Sign up for free eBooks

How would you like to receive notice whenever a brand new eBook is available to download for free? All you have to do is follow one link and Culinary Canary will be there to swoop in and drop off a notice for the newest eBook full of recipes to keep you excited about what you eat.

http://eepurl.com/FFncf

and we'll let you know exactly when the newest eBook is ready for you to take advantage of, with no spam or unnecessary emails clogging your inbox

.

What You Need To Know About Crepes Recipes

Introduction

The crepe has become a favorite international food item since its creation over a century ago. Its origins lie in France and from there, it has since become a hit and is now enjoyed all across the world, with everything from clubs and events being made to honor this delicious treat. A crepe is a type of thin pancake that can be made with various types of fillings and can be served in a breakfast, lunch or dinner setting. Lunch and dinner crepes, which are categorized as savory, consist of ingredients such as eggs, ham, cheese, mushrooms and artichoke. Breakfast crepes are generally served with sweeter ingredients, such as syrup, Nutella spreads, and various soft fruits cut into slices or small bits.

The common ingredients that Crepes are made from include eggs, flour, milk, butter and small amount of salt but can be made with different types of mixes. For example, one type of mix is a buckwheat crepes batter which can be more of a challenge to make, but many crepe enthusiasts find it to be tastier.

One method of making crepes is to roll the crepe and lightly bake, fry or sauté it for a different taste. The best part about crepes is that they can be filled with just about any ingredient and have numerous taste profiles for all kinds of occasions. You can make your crepe however you want; it all relies and you imagination and your personal preferences when it comes to taste.

Crepes have remained popular in France since their creation to this very day and it is extremely common to find them at shops and restaurants throughout the country. Crepes are so beloved that there are actually different forms of Crepe shops that can be found throughout Europe. One of the more popular shops that can be found is a creperie. A creperie is a standalone restaurant that serves crepes in the form of fast food since it is a faster alternative to order crepes on the go. It sure beats that sausage whatever muffin you might've been eating on your way to work.

On the second day of February every year, the French celebrate Candlemas, or as the French call it "La Chandeleur". People in America more commonly refer to this holiday as Crepe day. Candlemas is a Catholic holiday in which the people celebrate the purification of the Virgin Mary and the birth of Baby Jesus and also happen to feast on a ridiculous amount of crepes. While these two may not seem related, tradition is tradition. Another tradition is told that if you can catch a crepe that you flip with your recessive hand while holding a coin in your dominant hand during Candlemas, you and your family will be prosperous for the remainder of the year. Various French proverbs exist for Candlemas and some people have linked the similarities to the American holiday "Groundhog Day".

If you enjoy a sweet pastry-like delicacy or a savory concoction with meat, the crepe may be the French food for you. There are many reasons to try crepes, but they almost always add up to one similar answer: they always taste fantastic!

History

Crepes have enjoyed a long history, dating back to the Roman era. It wasn't until the 15th century that the crepe recipe was perfected in the Brittany region of France. Over time, the French began to enjoy sweet white flour crepes that were primarily served with coffee during breakfast or as an after dinner dessert item. The dessert would soon be revolutionized in a fortunate cooking accident. In 1895 Henri Charpentier, the nephew of the famous chef Escoffier who owned the famous Cafe de Paris, would make history. One night, the Prince of Wales was visiting the cafe and requested a crepe for his after dinner dessert. Feeling anxious to meet the Prince's high standard, Henri hurried to the kitchen to prepare a crepe fit for a prince. He filled the crepe with an orange sauce flambé and named it the Suzette to honor the Prince's female companion. In time the Crepe Suzette would become the most famous crepe dessert in the land. Sounds like a fairy tale right?

Now, different crepe variations have appeared across the world. Mexico enjoys the sope, a crepe like delicacy topped with syrup. Africa has their own incarnation, the injera, and India has the dosa. Almost all incarnations have some form of sliced fruit and sugar added to the mix. Henri Charpentier retired after creating his now world famous delicacy and his crepe creation has remained popular ever since.

Benefits of Making Crepes

There are some benefits to eating crepes. How could a sugary dessert have any benefits? Listed below are some examples of how eating crepes could be beneficial to your diet and lifestyle:

The Crepe Shouldn't be Fatty And Neither Should You

Crepes have typically been known to be low in fat. A 10 inch crepe often contains only 3 grams of total fat and only contains 1gram of saturated fat. Your body requires normal levels of fat for general health. However, saturated fat is a type of fat that can be harmful to your health. Consuming over 16 grams of saturated fat within a 24 hour time frame can have negative effects on your health if this habit is continued over time.

The advantage to eating crepes is that they contain very low levels of saturated fat. Having a crepe for breakfast or dessert at night can be much better for your health than having a sugary cereal or eating a fatty dessert. Avoiding heart attacks, strokes, and high cholesterol can be done by keeping an eye on how much saturated fat you consume per day and eating crepes can help you keep your saturated fat levels low.

Process less Processed Foods

Most food items you find on the marketplace today have been processed in one form or another. Preservatives add shelf life but take away healthy nutrients that are important to your diet. A positive to eating homemade crepes is that if you use all natural ingredients in your recipe, you are avoiding the preservatives other breakfast items might contain.

Use organic fruit slices when making a crepe or use grass fed meats for a healthier alternative to other choices you'll find in grocery stores or on a fast food menu. By creating the crepe at home, you are helping push your meal to be fresh and healthy when it comes time to eat while also avoiding negative eating habits such as eating a meal high in sodium, high in fat, or high in processed ingredients

Friendly Fruits and Vegetables

Fruit intake is always an important aspect to anyone's diet that often times goes overlooked. With crepes, that can be changed depending on what your preferences are in the fruit and vegetable kingdoms.

One of the great things about crepes is the interchangeable recipes that let you add just about whatever you want to a recipe. Listing out the number of nutrients and vitamins you'll get from increasing your fruit and vegetable intake on top of listing out the benefits could take forever. You can rest easier knowing that you'll be helping prevent diseases and improving the overall health of you and your family

Eating Crepes, Shedding Pounds

Crepes can be a great meal item or treat if you're trying to lose weight as well. The low calorie count and ability to fill your crepe with all kinds of beneficial ingredients is a much better alternative to desserts or even some meals that you might think of consuming.

Bodybuilders also often make their own type of crepe called "The bodybuilder's crepe." The crepe is traditionally made with whey protein powder, flavoring of choice, egg whites and protein filled content such as peanut butter and oats. This type of crepe is jam packed full of protein and is good for muscle building.

Whether you're looking to lose weight or add some protein to your diet, a crepe can be a great option to change up your meal and improve your health at the same time.

Caution for Crepes

With positives there always comes negatives. While the negatives in crepes may not make a large list, they are still worth noting.

Sugar count can sometimes be high in crepes depending on the recipe. For some people who are sensitive to sugar, such as diabetics or people trying to lose weight, you may need to watch what you put in your crepe.

Some versions of crepes can be fried which is also negative to your health in large consumptions. Fried foods have large amounts of fat in them and can lead to health problems such as obesity, heart problems and more.

These type of crepes may taste great, but always be sure to eat fried crepes as a "cheat day" kind of treat and not as your regular after lunch snack.

Crepes are such a diverse food item with a rich history. It's no wonder that the item has been celebrated by people all over the world. Crepes can fit just about any lifestyle and diet with its interchangeable recipes. Now grab your ingredients and get crepe-ing and remember, check out our other books for more meal and ingredient ideas, follow us on Facebook or sign up to our mailing list for more free eBooks, and have fun with these recipes and email us at culinarycanary@gmail.com for feedback or suggestions for our next book.

Crepes Recipes

Basic Crepes

Time: 20 minutes

Yield: 8 servings

Here's the building blocks. The foundation. The Big Bang of crepes. Without this, there is nothing (unless you go out and buy premade crepes, but that's no fun).

INGREDIENTS:

1 cup all-purpose flour
1/4 cup egg substitute *2 eggs*
1/2 cup milk
1/2 cup water
1/4 teaspoon salt
2 tablespoons oil
1 tablespoon butter

DIRECTIONS:

1. In a bowl, beat together flour and eggs. Add milk and water, mixing well. Put in salt and oil and whisk until smooth.
2. In a large mixing bowl, whisk together the flour and the eggs. Gradually add in the milk and water, stirring to combine. Add the salt and butter; beat until smooth.
3. To prepare crepes, melt butter in a large skillet. Pour 1/4 cup of batter and quickly swivel pan around to cover bottom. Once edges begin to brown, use a spatula to loosen and flip crepe over. Cook other side and additional 15 seconds. Place wax paper between each crepe to avoid sticking.

Buttermilk Crepes

Time: 45 minutes

Yield: 12 servings

What's the difference between these crepes and regular crepes? These crepes you'll find are fluffier and richer and are more suitable for dessert crepes.

INGREDIENTS:

1/3 cup egg substitute
1 - 1/2 cup coconut flour
1 cup buttermilk
1/4 sugar white sugar
1/4 cup brown sugar
3 tablespoons Earth Balance butter
1 teaspoon vanilla extract
1/2 teaspoon cinnamon
1/2 teaspoon nutmeg
1/2 teaspoon salt
1 tablespoon butter

DIRECTIONS:

1. In a large bowl, add egg substitute, coconut flour, buttermilk, white and brown sugar, Earth Balance butter, vanilla, cinnamon, nutmeg, and salt. Whisk together until smooth.
2. To prepare crepes, melt butter in a large skillet. Pour 1/4 cup of batter and quickly swivel pan around to cover bottom. Once edges begin to brown, use a spatula to loosen and flip crepe over. Cook other side and additional 15 seconds. Place wax paper between each crepe to avoid sticking.

Beer Batter Crepes

Time: 3 minutes

Yield: 12 crepes

These crepes are appropriate for lunches and desserts if you prefer your crepes to have a bit of additional taste.

INGREDIENTS:

1/3 cup, egg substitute

1 cup milk

1 cup lager beer

1 - 3/4 cups coconut flour

1 pinch salt

2 tablespoons vegetable oil

2 tablespoons butter

DIRECTIONS:

1. Whisk together egg substitute, milk, and lager in a large bowl. Slowly whisk in flour and add salt and oil. Mix thoroughly. Let batter stand for at least an hour.
2. To prepare crepes, melt butter in a large skillet. Pour 1/4 cup of batter and quickly swivel pan around to cover bottom. Once edges begin to brown, use a spatula to loosen and flip crepe over. Cook other side and additional 30 seconds. Place wax paper between each crepe to avoid sticking.

Banana Crepes

Time: 15 minutes

Yield: 6 servings

The sweet flavor of bananas combined with their texture makes them a perfect crepe candidate. A simple recipe to get you started, but still tastes pretty great.

INGREDIENTS:

1 cup coconut flour
1/4 cup confectioners' sugar
2 eggs
1 cup milk
3 tablespoons butter, melted
1 teaspoon maple syrup
1/4 teaspoon salt
1/4 cup butter
1/4 cup packed brown sugar
1 teaspoon vanilla extract
1/4 teaspoon ground cinnamon
1/4 teaspoon ground nutmeg
1/4 cup heavy cream
6 bananas, halved lengthwise
1 container Cool Whip

DIRECTIONS:

1. In a large bowl, sift sugar and flour. Add eggs, milk, butter, syrup, and salt and whisk until smooth.
2. Sift flour and powdered sugar into a mixing bowl. Add eggs, milk, butter, vanilla, and salt; beat until smooth.
3. To prepare crepes, melt butter in a large skillet. Pour 1/4 cup of batter and quickly swivel pan around to cover bottom. Once edges begin to brown, use a spatula to loosen and flip crepe over. Cook other side and additional 15 seconds. Place wax paper between each crepe to avoid sticking.
4. In a small saucepan, melt butter. Whisk in sugar and cinnamon. Stir in cream and add bananas letting them cook for 3 - 4 minutes. Set aside
5. Place one banana half in each crepe. Fold in half, drizzle over with banana sauce and a dollop of Cool Whip.
6. Melt 1/4 cup butter in a large skillet. Stir in brown sugar, 1/4 teaspoon cinnamon and nutmeg. Stir in cream and cook until slightly thickened. Add half the bananas at a time to skillet; cook for 2 to 3 minutes, spooning sauce over them. Remove from heat.
7. Roll a crepe around each banana half and place on serving platter. Spoon sauce over crepes. Top with whipped cream and a pinch of cinnamon.

French Crepes

Time: 30 minutes

Yield: 12 servings

These French toast-like crepes are perfect for converting crepe naysayers. If you'd like, top with a bit of maple syrup or fruit.

INGREDIENTS:

1 cup all-purpose flour

1 teaspoon brown sugar

1/4 teaspoon salt

3 eggs

2 cups milk

1 teaspoon vanilla extract

2 tablespoons butter, melted

DIRECTIONS:

1. In a bowl, whisk together flour, sugar, and salt. In a separate bowl, beat together eggs, milk, and vanilla. Mix dry ingredients slowly together with wet ingredients. Stir in butter.
2. To prepare crepes, melt butter in a large skillet. Pour 1/4 cup of batter and quickly swivel pan around to cover bottom. Once edges begin to brown, use a spatula to loosen and flip crepe over. Cook other side and additional 15 seconds. Place wax paper between each crepe to avoid sticking.

Creamy Strawberry Crepes

Time: 30 minutes

Yield: 12 servings

These mouthwatering, creamy, and sweet crepes are perfect for a breakfast where you feel like you need to treat yourself.

INGREDIENTS:

1/3 cup egg substitute

1/2 cup almond milk

1/2 cup water

3 tablespoons butter, melted

3/4 cup all-purpose flour

1/2 teaspoon salt

1/2 cup icing sugar

1 tablespoon lemon juice

1 teaspoon lemon zest

1/2 teaspoon vanilla extract

Pinch of cinnamon

1 container Cool Whip

4 cups sliced strawberries

DIRECTIONS:

1. Place egg substitute, almond milk, water, butter, flour, and salt in a bowl and mix until smooth.
2. To prepare crepes, melt butter in a large skillet. Pour 1/4 cup of batter and quickly swivel pan around to cover bottom. Once edges begin to brown, use a spatula to loosen and flip crepe over. Cook other side and additional 15 seconds. Place wax paper between each crepe to avoid sticking.
3. In a bowl, combine sugar, vanilla, cinnamon, Cool Whip, lemon zest and juice. Fold in strawberries.
4. Fill crepes with two tablespoons of strawberry cream mixture down the middle. Fold burrito style. Spoon mixture on top of crepes.

Vegan Crepes

Time: 20 minutes

Yield: 4 servings

Crepes often contain milk, eggs, and butter, and for a vegan, these items are definitely off the list. Instead, you can use substitutes and get your vegan friends in on the fun.

INGREDIENTS:

1/2 cup almond milk
1/2 cup water
1/4 cup melted Earth Balance butter
1/2 tablespoon stevia
2 teaspoons pure vanilla extract
1 cup coconut flour
1/4 teaspoon salt
1 tablespoon Earth Balance butter

DIRECTIONS:

1. In a bowl, add almond milk, water, Earth Balance butter, stevia, vanilla, flour, and salt. Mix thoroughly. Refrigerate for at least 2 hours.
2. To prepare crepes, melt butter in a large skillet. Pour 1/4 cup of batter and quickly swivel pan around to cover bottom. Once edges begin to brown, use a spatula to loosen and flip crepe over. Cook other side and additional 15 seconds. Place wax paper between each crepe to avoid sticking.

Fruity Chocolate Crepes

Time: 10 minutes

Yield: 4 servings

Whoa, a chocolate crepe? That's right, thanks to Nutella. With a Nutella spread and extra ingredients, this crepe can be a snack for brunch or a quick breakfast on the go.

INGREDIENTS:

1 cup Nutella

4 crepes

Half a pint strawberries, chopped

1 container Cool Whip

DIRECTIONS:

1. Spread 3 tablespoons of Nutella on each crepe. Spoon some strawberries along the middle.
2. Fold and top with whipped cream and sprinkling of cocoa powder.

Crepes with Spinach, Bacon and Mushroom Filling

Time: 20 minutes

Yield: 4 servings

These crepes are a mouthful of crunchy, tasty, and healthy elements that combine to give you the first surprise in your lunch crepe-ing career.

INGREDIENTS:

1 recipe Basic Crepes

6 slices turkey bacon
1 tablespoon unsalted butter
1/2 pound portabella mushrooms, sliced

3 tablespoons unsalted butter
1/4 cup all-purpose flour
1 cup heavy cream
1 package fresh baby spinach
1 tablespoon fresh cilantro, minced
2 tablespoons grated Parmesan cheese
Salt and pepper to taste

DIRECTIONS:

1. Prepare Basic Crepe Recipe according to directions. Set aside and keep warm.
2. In a large skillet, melt butter. Fry bacon until browned. Crumble and set aside.
3. In the same skillet, add oil and mushrooms and cook for 4 minutes.
4. Place bacon in a large, deep skillet. Cook over medium-high heat until evenly brown. Drain, crumble and set aside. Reserve about 1 tablespoon drippings, add 1 tablespoon butter, and sauté mushrooms.
5. In a saucepan over medium heat, melt butter. Add flour and whisk until a paste forms. Pour in heavy cream and stir until it begins to thicken. Add bacon, mushrooms, spinach, cilantro, cheese, salt and pepper. Cook until spinach had wilted slightly, about 7 - 10 minutes.
6. Place a crepe on a plate and spoon spinach mix along the middle. Fold over and enjoy.

South-western Crepes

Time: 20 minutes

Yield: 7 servings

These crepes have a great filling that tastes just like what you might find in your restaurant around the corner. Add in a desired sauce to cover your meat mixture if you'd like, but don't overdo it! Crepes are a bit more delicate than your average slice of bread.

INGREDIENTS:

1 lb. ground pork

2 tablespoons oil

1 red onion, diced

1 red bell peppers, diced

2 cups button mushrooms, sliced

1/4 cup cilantro, finely chopped

1/2 teaspoon garlic powder

1 cup all-purpose flour

1 egg

2 cups almond milk

DIRECTIONS:

1. In a skillet, heat oil. Add ground pork and cook for 5 minutes. Mix in onion, bell pepper, mushrooms, garlic powder and cilantro and continue cooking until meat has browned. Set aside.
2. In a bowl, mix together flour, egg, and milk.
3. To prepare crepes, melt butter in a large skillet. Pour 1/4 cup of batter and quickly swivel pan around to cover bottom. Once edges begin to brown, use a spatula to loosen and flip crepe over. Cook other side and additional 15 seconds. Place wax paper between each crepe to avoid sticking.
4. Place a crepe on a plate, spoon meat mixture in the middle and fold over.

Olive and Chicken Curry Crepes

Time: 15 minutes

Yield: 6 to 8 servings

Just when you think you've been surprised by crepes enough, here's another one to keep your taste buds on alert. For anyone who says crepes can't be a lunch or dinner, serve this and watch the look of defeat slowly dawn on their face.

INGREDIENTS:

CREPES

1 1/2 cups all-purpose flour

2 1/2 cups milk

3 eggs, beaten

2 tablespoons vegetable oil

1/2 teaspoon salt

FILLING

1/4 cup oil

1 cup diced onion

2 tablespoons all-purpose flour

1 teaspoon salt

3/4 teaspoon curry powder

1/4 teaspoon smoked paprika

3/4 cup heavy cream

1/2 cup chicken broth

3/4 cup Kalamata olives, finely chopped

3 cups chicken breast, cooked and shredded

1/4 cup cheddar cheese

1/2 cup salsa

DIRECTIONS:

1. In a bowl, mix together milk, flour, eggs, oil, and salt.
2. To prepare crepes, melt butter in a large skillet. Pour 1/4 cup of batter and quickly swivel pan around to cover bottom. Once edges begin to brown, use a spatula to loosen and flip crepe over. Cook other side and additional 15 seconds. Place wax paper between each crepe to avoid sticking. Set aside.
3. In a large skillet, heat up oil. Sauté onion for 3 minutes. Add flour, salt, curry, and paprika and mix well. Pour in broth and add olives and chicken and stir well.
4. Preheat oven to 375 degrees F.
5. Spoon chicken mixture onto middle of crepe. Fold burrito style. Lay seal down in a casserole dish. Pour over salsa and sprinkle cheese on top.
6. Bake for 12 - 15 minutes. Serve hot.

Indian Crepes

Time: 20 minutes

Yield: 6 servings

These Indian crepes have that hint of flavor that you need that will match up perfectly with most Indian dishes you can think to stuff these with. Try to keep the food you wrap in these crepes on the drier side, since a curry wouldn't work so well leaking all over your floors.

INGREDIENTS:

1 cup all-purpose flour

1 cup water

1 egg

2 tablespoons oil

1 pinch salt

1 tablespoon caraway seeds

1/2 teaspoon cumin

Yogurt, mint as toppings, optional

DIRECTIONS:

1. In a bowl, mix together flour and water. Mix in egg. Add oil, salt, caraway seeds, and cumin and whisk together until smooth.
2. To prepare crepes, melt butter in a large skillet. Pour 1/4 cup of batter and quickly swivel pan around to cover bottom. Once edges begin to brown, use a spatula to loosen and flip crepe over. Cook other side and additional 15 seconds. Place wax paper between each crepe to avoid sticking.
3. Fold crepes and serve with yogurt and mint.

Vanilla Crepes

Time: 20 minutes

Yield: 12 crepes

Need a crepe to wrap your dessert in and the buttermilk crepe just isn't doing it? These vanilla crepes have that bit of natural flavor to add that little bit of extra to your crepes.

INGREDIENTS:

1 - 1/2 cup almond milk

3 egg yolks

2 tablespoons vanilla extract

1 1/2 cups all-purpose flour

2 tablespoons brown sugar

1/2 teaspoon salt

5 tablespoons butter, melted

Maple syrup, whipped cream as toppings, optional

DIRECTIONS:

1. In a bowl, place milk, egg yolks, and vanilla. Slowly mix in flour, sugar, salt, and butter. Mix until smooth.
2. To prepare crepes, melt butter in a large skillet. Pour 1/4 cup of batter and quickly swivel pan around to cover bottom. Once edges begin to brown, use a spatula to loosen and flip crepe over. Cook other side and additional 15 seconds. Place wax paper between each crepe to avoid sticking.
3. Fold over and drizzle with maple syrup and top with a dollop of whipped cream.

Egg White Crepes

Time: 5 minutes

Yield: 4 servings

If you're looking for a bit of extra protein from your crepe without adding calories, look to the egg white crepe. This bad boy is perfect for those looking to lose or maintain weight.

INGREDIENTS:

1/2 cup whole wheat flour

2 egg whites

1/2 cup soy milk

1 pinch salt

1 tablespoon vegetable oil

1/4 cup fresh strawberries, chopped
1/4 cup fresh blueberries
1 tablespoon confectioners' sugar for dusting

DIRECTIONS:

1. In a bowl, whisk together flour, egg whites, milk, salt, and oil until fully combined.
2. To prepare crepes, melt butter in a large skillet. Pour 1/4 cup of batter and quickly swivel pan around to cover bottom. Once edges begin to brown, use a spatula to loosen and flip crepe over. Cook other side and additional 15 seconds. Place wax paper between each crepe to avoid sticking.
3. Fold over crepes. Sprinkle over with berries and sugar.

Strawberry Chocolate Crepes

Time: 10 minutes

Yield: 4 servings

If you're looking for a dessert crepe that brings a bit of natural fruit flavor along with the expected sweet sensation, this crepe is a great option.

INGREDIENTS:

CREPES

1 egg, beaten

1/4 cup almond milk

1/3 cup water

1/4 teaspoon vanilla extract

1 tablespoon vegetable oil

2/3 cup all-purpose flour

1/4 teaspoon white sugar

1 pinch salt

1 tablespoon butter

FILLING

1/2 cup semisweet chocolate chips

1 cup sliced fresh strawberries

1 cup heavy cream

2 cups confectioner's sugar

DIRECTIONS:

1. In a bowl, place egg, almond milk, water, vanilla, and oil. Mix well.
2. In a separate bowl, which together flour, sugar, and salt. Slowly whisk in dry ingredients to wet ingredients until fully incorporated.
3. To prepare crepes, melt butter in a large skillet. Pour 1/4 cup of batter and quickly swivel pan around to cover bottom. Once edges begin to brown, use a spatula to loosen and flip crepe over. Cook other side and additional 15 seconds. Place wax paper between each crepe to avoid sticking.
4. In a bowl, place sugar and heavy cream. Using an electric mixer, whisk consistently for about 5 minutes or when cream thicken and has the consistency of whipped cream.
5. Place chocolate chips in a microwavable bowl. Microwave for 90 seconds. Mix lightly.
6. Place crepe on a plate. Spread chocolate down the middle and lay strawberries on top of chocolate.
7. Roll crepes and top with a dollop of whipped cream and drizzle with remaining chocolate.

Eggless Crepes

Time: 10 minutes

Yield: 16 – 6 inch crepes

If you're for a bit thinner and crispier crepe, removing the eggs from the ingredient list can accomplish your goal without sacrificing the structural integrity or taste.

INGREDIENTS:

1/2 cup almond milk

2/3 cup water

1/4 cup butter, melted

1 tablespoon honey

1 cup all-purpose flour

1 tablespoon brown sugar

1/4 teaspoon salt

1 tablespoon butter

DIRECTIONS:

1. In a bowl, place milk, water, butter, and honey and mix well. In a separate bowl, whisk together flour, sugar, and salt.
2. Slowly whisk flour mixture into wet mixture until fully combined. Refrigerate for at least 2 hours.
3. In a medium bowl, mix together milk, water, melted butter, and vanilla extract. In a small bowl, thoroughly mix flour, sugar, and salt. Whisk flour mixture into milk mixture until batter is smooth. Cover and refrigerate 2 hours.
4. To prepare crepes, melt butter in a large skillet. Pour 1/4 cup of batter and quickly swivel pan around to cover bottom. Once edges begin to brown, use a spatula to loosen and flip crepe over. Cook other side and additional 15 seconds. Place wax paper between each crepe to avoid sticking.

Chocolate Banana Crepes

Time: 10 minutes

Yield: 4 servings

These crepes are another dessert crepe that mix a natural fruit flavor with the sweetness of chocolate to reel everyone in.

INGREDIENTS:

Crepe Batter:

1/2 cup whole or 2% milk

1 - 1/2 tablespoons butter, melted

1 egg yolk

1 teaspoon maple syrup

1 tablespoon hazelnut butter

1 tablespoon cocoa

2 tablespoons confectioners' sugar

1/3 cup coconut flour

Chocolate Sauce:

1/2 tablespoon butter

1 tablespoon almond milk

1 tablespoon hazelnut butter

1 tablespoon cocoa

2 tablespoons confectioner's sugar

2 ripe bananas, sliced

DIRECTIONS:

1. In a bowl, place milk, butter, egg yolk, maple syrup, and hazelnut butter. Mix well.
2. Whisk in cocoa powder then sugar until fully combined.
3. Slowly whisk in coconut flour until mixed in completely. Set aside.
4. In a small saucepan, melt butter. Add milk and hazelnut butter and whisk until butter has melted. Whisk in sugar and cocoa and reduce heat to low.
5. To prepare crepes, melt butter in a large skillet. Pour 1/4 cup of batter and quickly swivel pan around to cover bottom. Once edges begin to brown, use a spatula to loosen and flip crepe over. Cook other side and additional 30 seconds. Place wax paper between each crepe to avoid sticking.
6. On a plate, place crepe and add a few banana slices and drizzle a tablespoon of the chocolate sauce over the bananas. Fold over and sprinkle lightly with cocoa powder.

Orange-Anise Crepes

Time: 10 minutes

Yield: 6 servings

If you're looking for a bit of tang from your crepes, this recipe is guaranteed to deliver. Add some slices of mandarin or orange on top if you really enjoy the taste of orange!

INGREDIENTS:

2 cartons egg substitute

1 cup almond milk

3/4 cup orange juice

1 tablespoon caraway seeds, crushed

1 cup all-purpose flour

2 tablespoons butter, divided

Icing sugar, for dusting

DIRECTIONS:

1. In a bowl, place all ingredients, but butter, and beat well. Refrigerate for at least 8 hours.
2. To prepare crepes, melt butter in a large skillet. Pour 1/4 cup of batter and quickly swivel pan around to cover bottom. Once edges begin to brown, use a spatula to loosen and flip crepe over. Cook other side and additional 15 seconds. Place wax paper between each crepe to avoid sticking.
3. Sprinkle with icing sugar if desired.

Banana and Strawberry Yogurt Crepes

Time: 15 minutes

Yield: 8 crepes

These crepes are a great option for those healthy eaters in your life. Gaining the nutrients from the strawberries and bananas as well as the digestive benefits of the yogurt is guaranteed to keep your healthy eaters going throughout the day.

INGREDIENTS:

1 - 1/2 cup almond milk

3/4 cup flour

1/4 cup egg substitute

2 tablespoons agave syrup, divided
1 (8 ounce) container strawberry yogurt
1 banana, diced

1/4 cup strawberries, diced

1/4 teaspoon cinnamon

DIRECTIONS:

1. In a bowl, add almond milk, flour, egg substitute, and agave syrup and whisk together. Set aside
2. In a large skillet, heat up oil. Spoon in 1/4 cup batter and immediately swirl skillet so batter can cover entire bottom.
3. Cook for about 45 - 60 seconds. Use a spatula to loosen crepe and turn over. Cook other side for another 15 seconds. Place wax paper between every crepe so they don't stick.
4. In a bowl, whisk together yogurt, cinnamon, and agave syrup. Stir in banana and diced strawberries.
5. On each crepe, spread 2 heaping tablespoons of mixture. Fold up bottom and roll from left to right and serve.

How can you help Culinary Canary?

We would love to get your feedback about our book: Love the recipes in our books? Love the comedic styling of our writer? We'd love if you could leave a short review on Amazon of what you thought of the book. Not only does this help Culinary Canary fly as high as we possibly can, it also helps us improve book to book. If you want to write a review, all you've got to do is go to the same page you bought the book, click the review button, and leave a review. Thanks!

Free eBooks!

How would you like to receive notice whenever a brand new eBook is available to download for free? All you have to do is follow one link and Culinary Canary will be there to swoop in and drop off a notice for the newest eBook full of recipes to keep you excited about what you eat.

http://eepurl.com/FFncf

and we'll let you know exactly when the newest eBook is ready for you to take advantage of, with no spam or unnecessary emails clogging your inbox.

February's Golden Canary!

Starting with the month of February, Culinary Canary's going to be having a new contest each month to determine which of our readers deserves the coveted Yellow Canary!

Each book will contain a secret ingredient. With a minimum of 5 secret ingredients, it's up to you to create a dish that uses all of the ingredients; the more secret ingredients, the better! When you've made a dish, take a picture of it and send it in to Culinary Canary's Facebook page along with the recipe. The winner of each month's contest will receive a $50 Amazon gift card, their recipe featured in one of Culinary Canary's books, and a chance to win a Kindle Fire HDX!

This book's secret ingredient is:

<u>Baby Spinach</u>

Printed in Great Britain
by Amazon